After Advent

A Guide for Daily Reflection

Rev. Dr. A. René Whitaker

After Advent

Published by Whitaker Press

Cover design by Kraig Mentor
All rights reserved.

ISBN- 13-978-0-9976216-4-8

Dedication

This book is dedicated to all the women and men of faith upon whose shoulders I stand. They provided me with guidance, courage, strength and hope through all the joys and sorrows of this life. Thank you for sharing your lives with the world.

TABLE OF CONTENTS

Introduction

The poems on the following pages tell stories of faith, hope
and love. They include moments of heartache and happiness.
My hope is that they connect us together in ways new and
old. As you move through the days, I invite you to read
and ponder. Perhaps you will write you own reflection of
the part of your journey which unfolds today.

A Present Glimmer
What glimmers in the distance?
Is it hope or faith or love?
Perhaps we see starshine or fireflies.
Maybe it is merely a headlight
or better yet two.
Or is it the glow of a porchlight
which was lit just for you?
Yes, a glimmer it is, not quite
A twinkle or spark.
But it lights the way to the future
leading us out of the dark.

John 1:1-5

In the beginning was the Word, and the Word was with God,
and the Word was God. He was in the beginning with God. All
things came into being through him, and without him not one
thing came into being. What has come into being in him was life,
and the life was the light of all people. The light shines in the
darkness, and the darkness did not overcome it.

DAY ONE

After Advent

How do we prepare for life after Advent?
What do we expect when Emmanuel is sent?
We say, "God is with us" in the birth of this child.
We ask, "What can it mean?" as our thoughts run wild.
Bonhoeffer asked the question. The shepherds did as well.
With words of glory the angels sing.
With hope filled hearts we hear silver bells ring.
Our eyes open wide. We may find hope deep inside.
Will this year be different, and what would that mean?
Could there be earthly peace or is that just a dream?

If we kneel before the child with wonder and awe,
Will we remember the vision we hope we saw?
Can we know how the story should be told?
What expectations do we hold?
What will our anticipation bring?
Perhaps a few moments beyond any ordinary thing?
Or will we discover profound change in daily life
As we open to gratitude and let go of strife?

Yet even in the wondering I believe something new does appear
Heartache is diminished and joy blocks out our fear.
Does the journey lead to kindness and beyond bitter thought?
Are we released from our blindness?
So with renewed vision we are taught ... to wish
for more than a trinket or presents in a sleigh
As we turn our expectations to create a brand new way.
And although we are the same as we were yesterday.
We see with eyes made new so that together we may pray:
"Rejoice, rejoice believers and let your light shine through
The Christ child sits before us and all things are brand new."

DAY ONE, continued

After Advent

Luke 2:8-15

In that region there were shepherds living in the fields, keeping watch over their flock by night. Then an angel of the Lord stood before them, and the glory of the Lord shone around them, and they were terrified. But the angel said to them, "Do not be afraid; for see—I am bringing you good news of great joy for all the people: to you is born this day in the city of David a Savior, who is the Messiah, the Lord.

This will be a sign for you: you will find a child wrapped in bands of cloth and lying in a manger." And suddenly there was with the angel a multitude of the heavenly host, praising God and saying, "Glory to God in the highest heaven, and on earth peace among those whom he favors!" When the angels had left them and gone into heaven, the shepherds said to one another, "Let us go now to Bethlehem and see this thing that has taken place, which the Lord has made known to us."

What does Advent mean to you?

Have you been changed by the Advent journey?

What are your expectations along the way?

What did you discover about yourself
and your life of faith?

DAY TWO

Glory Enough

Glory enough for everyone; not just me and you.
Grace enough for all of us; not just a privileged few.
God's presence hidden by smoke and fire.
Our glory revealed through hope and desire.
We don't choose where the sun will shine.
Nor are we right to say, "God's only mine."
We plant the fields; yet we can't make things grow.
That's beyond the factors that we can know.
We didn't send Jesus here to save.
No, Jesus was a gift from beyond the grave.
Just like all the gifts of love and life.
God offers hope in the midst of strife.
What more is there for us to say?
God's glory is really here to stay.
No matter who we are or where we may roam.
It's God's glory that will surely,
Yes, surely God's glory will lead us home.

2 Corinthians 3:17-18

Now the Lord is the Spirit, and where the Spirit of the Lord is, there is freedom. And all of us, with unveiled faces, seeing the glory of the Lord as though reflected in a mirror, are being transformed into the same image from one degree of glory to another; for this comes from the Lord, the Spirit.

Can you believe that there is glory enough,
love enough for everyone?

Your friends? Your family? Neighbors? Gay or Straight?

People who do not look like you or who speak another language?

DAY THREE

Wait for Awhile

I'm just not quite sure what my prayer should be.
Do I ask for something as I hear the words, "Follow me"?
Shall I give everything up to go a new way.
Or sit and listen as I go through this unfolding bright day?
My ears are wide open and my heart yearns to know
What should I do and where must I go?
For right now at least the instructions are clear
And I'm not sure I like what I hear
"Wait" for awhile right where you are
Sit with your sorrows and don't travel too far.
It's not time to move to some place far or near.
You've been asked to stand still and encounter your fear
Of the past and the future of life as it's revealed
Every moment does count and the prophecy sealed
In the halls of heaven where the angels live
Like everyone else you may take as you give.
Take this cup that has been prepared for you
And then share it with others as you are asked to do.
But don't just run in circles or squares
Wait 'til you know the things you must dare.
You'll tell the stories of love, life and such.
If you follow when called, it can't be too much
To show that you care for the weak and the strong
It won't really matter if some days it seems wrong
Because the one God of all will work with what we give
To create a new world where others may live
With joy and peace deep inside
As we continue to learn that only together
In God shall we always abide.

DAY THREE, continued

Wait for Awhile

Psalm 27:14
Wait for the Lord; be strong, and let your heart take courage;
wait for the Lord.

What are you being called to do at this moment in your life?

Do you see a direction in front of you?

OR

Do you need to wait until a path is made clear?

DAY FOUR

When Winter Comes
When winter comes
Everything changes
Including the light which
Grows dimmer and brighter
All at the same time
As the evening turns to night
Houses begin to glow
The outside cools but we snuggle
Into the warmth of inside
And wait until the light returns

When winter comes
The landscape is barren
With a beauty all its own
Leaves have long blown away
The sky hangs lower
And the sun hides
earlier each day
We huddle inside our coats
And hats and gloves
And wait until the warmth comes again.

Genesis 1:3-5

Then God said, "Let there be light"; and there was light. And God saw that the light was good; and God separated the light from the darkness. God called the light Day, and the darkness he called Night. And there was evening and there was morning, the first day.

DAY Four, continued

When Winter Comes

Do you look forward to the coming of Winter?

Does the changing light impact your life?

How do you thrive as you huddle inside your coat/?

DAY FIVE

Because We Have Been
Enlightened by a shining sun.
Enlivened by a cup of tea.
We take heart because others
Have gone before us
Who sacrificed and surrendered
Their freedom without formation
Gregarious or solitary each life counted
Even if we don't know who they are
Because they lived and died
Without their voices being heard
outside their small circle of life.
Some travelled to Rome and back
Others only to the barn to milk the cow
Or perhaps there was not even a place
And no animal to provide sustenance
Those we have heard from through the centuries
Had the means to make a way
Many were lost to poverty and deprivation
Some rose by accident of grace
Others fell at the hands of enemies
Or perhaps a relative who suffered as well
We place meaning on the stories of the past
Whether or not that was how they meant to be
And so we will continue to move
And breathe in our own small circles
Even as we change the world
Simply because we have been.

DAY FIVE, continued

Because We Have Been

Matthew 5:1-9

When Jesus saw the crowds, he went up the mountain; and after he sat down, his disciples came to him. Then he began to speak, and taught them, saying:

'Blessed are the poor in spirit, for theirs is the kingdom of heaven.
'Blessed are those who mourn, for they will be comforted.
'Blessed are the meek, for they will inherit the earth.
'Blessed are those who hunger and thirst for righteousness,
    for they will be filled.
'Blessed are the merciful, for they will receive mercy.
'Blessed are the pure in heart, for they will see God.
'Blessed are the peacemakers, for they will be called
    children of God.

Who are the unsung heroes of your life?

What stories would you like to tell?

DAY SIX

Anger & Heartache

Anger and heartache often go hand in hand
They circle around and replace and reveal
The stories of death in life that show us what's real.

Yet we seek life beyond death.
We search for life made new.
It's this hope which carries us forward
As we seek to learn what's true.
So that we can move beyond and even rise above.
And in our rising we may discover
something we call true love
Still we may we kick off our feet from the dust
And curse the ground and world around
While we simply seek to find new trust.

Sometimes we scream.
.Other times we cry
And yet, the only true salvation is to trust and try
And try some more to go beyond and rise above
The only helpful answer is to speak the truth in love.

But who wants to hear the truth these days.
It gets lost in clutter and clouds our gaze
So we duck our heads and cover our eyes
Cause our fragile souls need a bigger disguise
Than just the stories that sometimes bring cries
Of joy but sorrow as well
There is nothing else more than these stories will tell
But often some see it one way and they see it another;
And then we forget she's a sister and he's our brother.

DAY SIX, continued

Anger & Heartache

In life and death and all this stuff
Cause somehow or other the truth isn't enough
To help us believe that the world is so complex
We just can't capture it all in a couple of texts
So we put on our masks and pretend it's okay
To lie or deceive to just get your way
And even when the light of truth shines on the path outside
Too many will hide since it is the light they cannot abide.

Isaiah 60:1-5

Arise, shine; for your light has come, and the glory of the Lord has risen upon you. For darkness shall cover the earth, and thick darkness the peoples; but the Lord will arise upon you, and his glory will appear over you. Nations shall come to your light, and kings to the brightness of your dawn.

Lift up your eyes and look around; they all gather together, they come to you; your sons shall come from far away, and your daughters shall be carried on their nurses' arms. Then you shall see and be radiant; your heart shall thrill and rejoice, because the abundance of the sea shall be brought to you, the wealth of the nations shall come to you.

What truth are you seeking today?

How will you know it is true?

DAY SEVEN

Oh My!

It isn't time to write anything profound
My words are jumbled
They only make some sound
That can't be quite discerned
Among the clatter of tires and trees
Rustling in the wind
This unsettled noise just clutters clarity
Yet I need to believe
and dream of faith and hope and pray for charity
Instead there was a memory of grandma
Long time gone
So I woke with a start sensing pain in my heart
And head and such
It makes me yearn for the simple
Kindness of her touch
But all that was heard were two simple words, "Oh my"
She said, "Oh my" is all.
And she listened and listened
Beyond the call
Still time marched on
Some couldn't look on my face
And see who I was a real person
Who feels disgraced.
They just didn't want to admit what was true.
The bully, the coward was given
the power to simply tell lies
Without any replies
And they believed them because
I was brand new
Yet it was over my life That the wild winds blew

DAY SEVEN continued

Oh My!

Soon anger or fear led the charge
Yes, it had to be me
Cause I stood up for myself
And it's true don't you see
For it's what any sane person would do
They came after me as I stood my ground
But soon after that there was no one around
To stand by me and say, "This is wrong."
Instead they simply joined in the throng
And cried: "Off with her head"
We know we'll be better unled
Then she walks on her way
With little to say,
"Just go to hell"
Cause I'm not gonna tell
I'm angry and it's ok
At least for another whole day.

Psalm 140

Deliver me, O Lord, from evildoers; protect me from those who are violent, who plan evil things in their minds and stir up wars continually. They make their tongue sharp as a snake's, and under their lips is the venom of vipers. Guard me, O Lord, from the hands of the wicked; protect me from the violent who have planned my downfall...I say to the Lord, 'You are my God; give ear, O Lord, to the voice of my supplications.'

Is there a time when you were hurt by a bully or a coward?

Were there people who stood up for you or with you along the way?

If so, give thanks for them and
pray for all involved to find healing and peace.

DAY EIGHT

When a Dream Dies
When a dream dies,
What does that mean?
Where to go next?
Where have we been?
Together and not
As the world twirls around
I can see everything
But can't hear a sound
Beyond the choir in my head
Cause I'm surrounded by angels
Fed with heavenly bread
The chorus is sad and glorious too
Not sure how to act
Or how I'll get through
This maze of feeling and fact
Yet I believe that I'll find what I lack.
I understand that hope trumps fear
But sometimes it seems to all but disappear
Then we remember that love conquers hate
And still there are moments when
It seems to hesitate
As we dither and doubt that its true
Our anxiety rises.
We forget what to do
Before and after the hour slips on past
As we pray for kindness and care to come fast
And stay even longer than this thing called hate
Which seems to pervade almost every debate

DAY EIGHT, continued

When a Dream Dies

Genesis 28:10-19

Jacob left Beer-sheba and went toward Haran. He came to a certain place and stayed there for the night, because the sun had set. Taking one of the stones of the place, he put it under his head and lay down in that place. And he dreamed that there was a ladder set up on the earth, the top of it reaching to heaven; and the angels of God were ascending and descending on it. And the Lord stood beside him and said, "I am the Lord, the God of Abraham your father and the God of Isaac; the land on which you lie I will give to you and to your offspring; and your offspring shall be like the dust of the earth, and you shall spread abroad to the west and to the east and to the north and to the south; and all the families of the earth shall be blessed in you and in your offspring. Know that I am with you and will keep you wherever you go, and will bring you back to this land; for I will not leave you until I have done what I have promised you."

Then Jacob woke from his sleep and said, "Surely the Lord is in this place—and I did not know it!" And he was afraid, and said, "How awesome is this place! This is none other than the house of God, and this is the gate of heaven." So Jacob rose early in the morning, and he took the stone that he had put under his head and set it up for a pillar and poured oil on the top of it. He called that place Bethel; but the name of the city was Luz at the first.

What do you need today to overcome any obstacles holding you down?

Who can help you along the journey?

What one thing can you do today to renew your dream?

DAY NINE

Good Enough for Mercy
I stare into the abyss
And then I cast my lot
I wonder if I will simply disappear
Or seek forever forward

No matter what may come
The day shines its beauty
But I don't care.
For it seems this beauty
Is not mine to share
So all I can do is stare
Into heartache and worry.

The glory of the day can't
Seem to cast sorrow away
For this is what has been and will be
Beauty and heartache
Danger and desire
Always striving
To be more and better
Than before.

What does that mean to be better?
Was I insufficient just yesterday?
Not quite good enough for mercy
Or even a margin of error?
Help me see it all as a way
That isn't less that we hoped.
Or not good enough to be forgiven

DAY NINE, continued

Good Enough for Mercy
Help me see it all as a way
That isn't less that we hoped.
Or not good enough to be forgiven
Because I know that I am
Grateful for this beauty
that I didn't cause
And a moment of peace
That doesn't pretend all is well ...
'Cause it isn't;
And Jesus already knew that to be true.
So I simply say, "Thank you."

Hebrews 4:14-16

Since, then, we have a great high priest who has passed through the heavens, Jesus, the Son of God, let us hold fast to our confession. For we do not have a high priest who is unable to sympathize with our weaknesses, but we have one who in every respect has been tested as we are, yet without sin. Let us therefore approach the throne of grace with boldness, so that we may receive mercy and find grace to help in time of need.

What does it mean to be better?

Is your life insufficient for mercy?

Why do believe that is so?

Where do you turn to remember grace, forgiveness and peace?

DAY TEN

First Place Enemies

What makes us enemies in the first place?
Do words separate without our knowing?
Do we categorize, characterize and criticize
some simply because they are different?
Or is it character which distinguishes who we are?
Perhaps we are different and adequate
and others wish we were not?
Is it caring about our differences that causes us
to be enemies?
Or is it that we just don't care
Who they are unless they are just like us?
But who are we?
Who are we in the eyes of God?
We are glorious & greedy.
We are arrogant yet angelic.
We are connected through and to infinity
Even while we are finite.
Mostly we are fragile.
Our egos can be wounded, our hearts can be broken
and our expectations cast aside as unworthy, unrealistic or wrong.
Too often it becomes us versus them
Or me better than you even though
We are all given birth by one
Creative force we name God.
What happens when our fragility overwhelms us
and our flaws are revealed even as gravity weighs us down?
What occurs when despair or deprivation makes us feel weak;
and we can't seem to learn that we need others even
after we have been taught to be independent.

DAY TEN, continued

First Place Enemies
Only in our differences can we learn that
We are more alike than we can begin to imagine.
And when we stand at the grave
We are no longer unique but thrust back into
The oneness of the creation
As particles of dust and ashes
to reform the stars from which we were born.
Even then all we can really say is "Thank You.
Thank you. Alleluia. Amen."

Matthew 5:44-45

But I say to you, Love your enemies and pray for those who perse-
cute you, so that you may be children of your Father in heaven; for he
makes his sun rise on the evil and on the good, and sends rain on the
righteous and on the unrighteous.

What makes us enemies in the first place?

How do you learn to love your enemies?

Who can help in your learning?

DAY ELEVEN

Words, Words, Words

Words, Words, Words
Too many words scrambled in my head.
Years of reading & thinking & wondering
What & why
Then leading people in the Word of worship.
Sometimes like Eliza there are simply too many words
So I can't hear the chorus of angelic voices.
Because everyone wants to share more words.
There is no separate self that can leave or lead our lives
Beyond where we are.
The past has formed us and frames who we are.
Our selves are neither false or true …
They are pieces and parts or parts and pieces
of the whole of who we have been,
And then they/we/I
become more than I was.
My defenses, your defenses
Keep us safe until
such a time when there is room
to be just who we are.
No more, no less.
We judge every moment
and yet often call it wrong.
Still every second is a manifested gift
that reveals where we have been.
We are never sure that
they will enable us to overcome
expectations of where
we will find ourselves tomorrow.

DAY ELEVEN, continued

Words, Words, Words
So we journey alone even as
We are on the road
Together
Intersecting and diverging
with friends and strangers
and then tomorrow
Something new will be begun.
Words, words, words … too many words.

John 1:1-5*

In the beginning was the Word, and the Word was with God, and the Word was God. The Word was in the beginning with God. All things came into being through the Word, and without the Word not one thing came into being. What has come into being in the Word was life, and the life was the light of all lpeople. The light shines in the deepest night, and the night did not overcome it.

What words do you use to describe your own life?

What words do you use to connect your life with others?

*Scripture from *The New Testament and Psalms: An Inclusive Version,* Oxford University Press, New York, New YOrk, 1995, 142.

DAY TWELVE

On the Way to Memphis
Sorrow settles in my bones and muscles and mind
Now the work of grief sits in the middle of joy
And here they go hand in hand even if that isn't what we wish for
But there is gratitude for the angels who are shedding tears
With and for me and for you too
And God blesses the 18th day (or whatever day this is for you)
and pronounces it good
And words of wonder continue to spill forth
Right alongside the tears
And I fly past the harvest fields filled with dust and energy
On the way to Memphis where music and madness
and perhaps even miracles await.

Genesis 1:26-31

Then God said, "Let us make humankind in our image, according to our likeness; and let them have dominion over the fish of the sea, and over the birds of the air, and over the cattle, and over all the wild animals of the earth, and over every creeping thing that creeps upon the earth." So God created humankind in his image, in the image of God he created them; male and female he created them. God blessed them, and God said to them, "Be fruitful and multiply, and fill the earth and subdue it; and have dominion over the fish of the sea and over the birds of the air and over every living thing that moves upon the earth."

God said, "See, I have given you every plant yielding seed that is upon the face of all the earth, and every tree with seed in its fruit; you shall have them for food. And to every beast of the earth, and to every bird of the air, and to everything that creeps on the earth, everything that has the breath of life, I have given every green plant for food." And it was so. God saw everything that he had made, and indeed, it was very good. And there was evening and there was morning, the sixth day.

DAY TWELVE, continued

On the Way to Memphis

For what are you grateful today?

For whom are you grateful today?

Can you name the miracles of life all around you?

DAY THIRTEEN

Notes We Cannot Hear
There are notes we cannot hear
When the sound just isn't clear
From without or here within
Or is it broken like my heart
And the music will not start to play again

Where did you go?
How have you been?
I'm wondering every day
Cause you voice is mute
And I can't compute or speak a sound

Still the thoughts continue
They go round and round
So I play or even pray
As I listen for the note, I cannot hear
Cause my dream did disappear
When you went away.

Perhaps some day
We will hear the music play
Together at last not alone
So that the music that's played
will remember you stayed in my heart
and soul and mind
Just forever be kind
Cause we will never rewind
The notes that forever were there.

DAY THIRTEEN, continued

Notes We Cannot Hear

Micah 6:8
   He has told you, O mortal, what is good; and what does the Lord require of you but to do justice, and to love kindness, and to walk humbly with your God?

Are you missing someone in your life?

Who were/are they?

Is there a story you would like to tell?

DAY FOURTEEN

Telling Time

"Only time will tell," we say
But the mountains don't count the days
Or weeks or hours
Only we human beings who believe
That somehow time is ours
To tell or break apart
Organizing to the end or punctuating at the start
reasons to be somewhere
at a particular moment in time
so that we place meaning here or there
and hope that it will rhyme
or at least give us a reason for what we do
right now or even then
as we mark our calendars with how or why
but most of all we want to know when
shall I arrive or depart
what time is the show
when did he break just your heart
The little and large are measured in time
A second, a week even a life lived sublime
Is marked and measured until
we run out of time and only then
Will we tell the tales to those left behind.

DAY FOURTEEN, continued

Telling Time

James 4:13-17

Come now, you who say, "Today or tomorrow we will go to such and such a town and spend a year there, doing business and making money." Yet you do not even know what tomorrow will bring. What is your life? For you are a mist that appears for a little while and then vanishes. Instead you ought to say, "If the Lord wishes, we will live and do this or that." As it is, you boast in your arrogance; all such boasting is evil. Anyone, then, who knows the right thing to do and fails to do it, commits sin.

What will you do with the time given to you today?

This week?

This month?

This year?

DAY FIFTEEN

The Outcome

We don't know the outcome or what there will be
A day without sunlight or an hour without electricity
Will the rain pour down at a funeral
or when we put on our wedding gown
May laughter unfold or tears fill our eyes
Whatever might happen will leave us surprised
The options are many; true choices are few.
We may decide what's for lunch,
but didn't see the wind as it blew
Our lives apart and back together again

There are times we may lose;
and other moments we will win
Even when the outcome allows us to shine
We can't always tell you that everything's fine

The stars may be bright and the plans come to be
As we call out to God to just hear our plea
Sometimes we must listen and look beyond what we see
Cause we don't know the outcome
or the details beyond right now
We can only look forward in hope
As we remember to say "thank you" and totally "Wow"!

DAY FIFTEEN, continued

The Outcome

1 Corinthians 13:12-13
For now we see in a mirror, dimly, but then we will see face to face. Now I know only in part; then I will know fully, even as I have been fully known. And now faith, hope, and love abide, these three; and the greatest of these is love.

What are you grateful for today?

What part of your life encourages you to say, "Wow!"

DAY SIXTEEN

Heading Back to Pittsburgh
So I'm heading back to Pittsburgh
I don't know what it means
But I'm wearing comfy clothes
A sweatshirt and some jeans.
The world around me is changing.
It will never be the same
I guess I'll just get ready
To learn the rules of this new game.

I'm heading back to Pittsburgh
To see how things will be
We'll hide some eggs for Easter and sing of victory.
What have we won I wonder
With a twinkle in my eye
We've won the right to live with love
Every moment till we die
This prize it isn't just for you
It's for all people everywhere.
I tell you since I know it's true.
Everyone can live in love
Until we say goodbye
And then beyond the grave
That love just keeps on giving
Believe it ... 'cause I just can't lie.

I'm heading back to Pittsburgh to preach the love of God
I wonder if it matters so many think it's odd
To talk of love and justice as though we really care.
No matter what they think it's a message I must share
Cause without this hope & promise
We'll all be really lost

DAY SIXTEEN, continued

Heading Back to Pittsburgh
So I'm heading back to Pittsburgh no matter what the cost
Cause everyday I'm given the breath of life you see
It's a miracle to ponder and a sign of victory.

So I'm heading back to Pittsburgh cause that's where I belong
And with every mile I drive I keep singing this same song
So let's head on back to Pittsburgh
And claim our victory cause tomorrow
Is another day with new miracles to see.

Inspired by *Victory in Jesus**
I heard an old, old story, how a Savior came from glory,
How He gave His life on Calvary to save a wretch like me;
I heard about His groaning, of His precious blood's atoning,
Then I repented of my sins and won the victory.

Chorus: O victory in Jesus, my Savior, forever.
He sought me and bought me with His redeeming blood;
He loved me ere I knew Him and all my love is due Him,
He plunged me to victory, beneath the cleansing flood.

I heard about His healing, of His cleansing pow'r revealing.
How He made the lame to walk again and caused the blind to see;
And then I cried, "Dear Jesus, Come and heal my broken spirit,"
And somehow Jesus came and bro't to me the victory.

How do you claim victory in your life today?

For whom can you offer a prayer of thanksgiving?

* "Victory in Jesus" was the final song E. M. Bartlett wrote. The hymn also became his best known and most embraced song. The song is an optimistic reminder of the hope of heaven. In the second stanza, there are references to the healing ministry of Christ.

DAY SEVENTEEN

Time Is

Time is the only thing that will help
And yet, it is relentless.
Perhaps there isn't enough time
To undo sorrow.
We may know that joy is out there
Somewhere or deep inside.
It pops up once in awhile or lasts even longer.

When tragedy strikes we say, "Give it time."
But it takes more than time to heal the pain.
Sometimes I'm not sure
If even Jesus can help.
Yet, where else shall we turn?

So I pray: "Help me Jesus 'cause I can't get up
And see what's on ahead."

So time ticks by as we wait to find that
trust has come back around
From where we don't know
Yet new life appears which may
more than simply astound
And so in time we must surely believe
That even now
The resurrection story is true.

So let's step in line and march with time
that's the best that you and I
and the rest of us can do.

Time Is

Ecclesiastes 3:1

For everything there is a season, and a time for every matter under heaven.

In what season of life do you find yourself today?

Are you prepared for life made new by the passage of time?

DAY EIGHTEEN

Gravity or Depravity
Gravity or depravity
Which one will it be?
An attitude of gratitude makes it easy to see.
Gravity is here and now
Depravity is dead
Bow down, give thanks and then lift up your head.

Look around. It's safe to do.
Gravity is your grace.
It's not too weak; it's not too strong.
We won't float off to outer space.

Gravity or depravity
Which one will it be?
Let's take the grace of gravity
setting old depravity free.

2 Corinthians 12:8-9
Three times I appealed to the Lord about this, that it would leave me, but he said to me, "My grace is sufficient for you, for power is made perfect in weakness." So, I will boast all the more gladly of my weaknesses, so that the power of Christ may dwell in me.

Let us remember -- Gravity is grace.

What does depravity mean to you today?

Where do you see the grace of gravity today?

DAY NINETEEN

Nevertheless
We are broken and made
Some are betrayed
We wander off course
The games have been played

The sorrow, the guilt
Infected our heart
We think we are lost
Even before we can start
But that's not the truth
Not even one bit
Life is for living
We don't want you to quit

Don't quit having hope
That a new day will shine
Don't quit seeking more
Even something divine
Not not, now ever
No matter how hard
Reach out for help
Even an inch or a yard
Beyond the place you
Stand right now
Pay close attention
And we'll show you how
To live and love
Perhaps laugh once more
Climb through that window
Or walk through the door
That leads to tomorrow

DAY NINETEEN, continued

Nevertheless
Don't stop with today
It will be different
If you move past dismay
To see the light
That shines oh so bright
Look past your worries
And step left or right
You can go back or
Even ahead
Each journey is different

Yet we all are led
To a new space if
We let it be
Something quite different
Even a surprise you see
That's how faith works
In mysterious ways
Beyond our control
For the rest of our days

Yes, we may doubt
Or get stuck in the grime
As long as we breathe
There is plenty of time
To try again and
See where to go
That's how it happens
That's how we grow

Wiser, stronger and
Filled with God's grace
There's no competition
This isn't a race

Nevertheless
There aren't any losers
We all win in the end
Cause it isn't our striving
On which we depend
Rather it's only a miracle
The nevertheless
Something inexplicable
I simply confess

Acceptance my child
For just who you are
Created in darkness
And blessed by a star
Which shines overhead
Throughout every time
A spectacular promise
That is truly sublime

Receive this gift of
Light filled with love
I share it with you
Yet it came from above

Above and beyond
The world that we see
It's more than enough
To fulfill your destiny
To live as a child
Of the creator of all
To share in the goodness
Of this special call

DAY NINETEEN, continued

Nevertheless

It's more than enough
To carry us through
The long days ahead

Beyond the world that we knew
And when day is done
We can just close our eyes
Cause whatever we find
Will have been a surprise

So with a whisper of hope
We say "thanks" and "amen"
Knowing that this is
How we begin once again

Romans 8:18-25

I consider that the sufferings of this present time are not worth comparing with the glory about to be revealed to us. For the creation waits with eager longing for the revealing of the children of God; for the creation was subjected to futility, not of its own will but by the will of the one who subjected it, in hope that the creation itself will be set free from its bondage to decay and will obtain the freedom of the glory of the children of God.

We know that the whole creation has been groaning in labour pains until now; and not only the creation, but we ourselves, who have the first fruits of the Spirit, groan inwardly while we wait for adoption, the redemption of our bodies. For in hope we were saved. Now hope that is seen is not hope. For who hopes for what is seen? But if we hope for what we do not see, we wait for it with patience.

DAY NINETEEN, continued

Nevertheless

How did life suprirse you today?

What is your hope for tomorrow?

From whom will you discover this hope?

DAY TWENTY

A Reflection on Lazarus

This holy week reflection is in response to a quote and question from Lent and Easter Wisdom from Thomas Merton, Day 41: "Imagine you are Lazarus risen from the dead. You are at table with Jesus and your sisters: Have you anything to say?" When I first read, I was sure I would sit there in shock and say nothing at all. Then I pondered this some more, and I wrote the following:

> If I were Lazarus raised from the dead,
>   I would weep because.
> Because it has happened to me again and again.
>   I was dead, and yet didn't know it.
> I would weep because I was a different person now,
>   And I'm not sure how to be.
>
> I would weep in glory and in awe.
>   I would weep because it is so hard to understand
>   for myself.
> And it is almost impossible to describe to others
>   Unless they have been raised too.
> I would weep because I am fragile
>   But mostly I would weep because
> I am grateful to be alive once again.
>   Life is something beyond belief, and I must weep.
>
> And then as the tears lay on my face
>   I would laugh out loud because.
> Simply because it is absurd this living again.
>   I remember feeling dead, but perhaps I wasn't.
> I laugh because it is ridiculous
>   To be brought back to life knowing at once
> I will surely die again.

DAY TWENTY, continued

A Reflection on Lazarus

But for now I am offered the chance to laugh
In the face of death and to know it is overcome.
I weep and I laugh because I am human, and
This is what I am truly called to do.
And whether together or apart
I sit at table with you and Jesus and all the rest
who live again today.

John 11:1-5

Now a certain man was ill, Lazarus of Bethany, the village of Mary and her sister Martha. Mary was the one who anointed the Lord with perfume and wiped his feet with her hair; her brother Lazarus was ill. So the sisters sent a message to Jesus, 'Lord, he whom you love is ill.' But when Jesus heard it, he said, 'This illness does not lead to death; rather it is for God's glory, so that the Son of God may be glorified through it.' Accordingly, though Jesus loved Martha and her sister and Lazarus, after having heard that Lazarus was ill, he stayed two days longer in the place where he was.

So imagine that you are Lazarus raised from the dead:

"What would you say?"

DAY TWENTY-ONE

The Four M's
Does it matter if we call it magic, medicine,
mystery or miracle?
Our minds are machines and not.
They are a mesmerizing, intertwining
Matrix of interconnections
Which we cannot see if the brain
Is simply set on the table by itself.
Once it is unplugged from our bodies
It is only a blob of blood and synapses
Which no longer flow as we would wish.

Ephesians 3:7-11

Of this gospel I have become a servant according to the gift of God's grace that was given to me by the working of his power. Although I am the very least of all the saints, this grace was given to me to bring to the Gentiles the news of the boundless riches of Christ, and to make everyone see what is the plan of the mystery hidden for ages in God who created all things; so that through the church the wisdom of God in its rich variety might now be made known to the rulers and authorities in the heavenly places. This was in accordance with the eternal purpose that God has carried out in Christ Jesus our Lord, in whom we have access to God in boldness and confidence through faith in him.

Does it matter what words we use?

What word would you use? Why?

DAY TWENTY-TWO

Swinging in the Park

We remember with joy
The days of swinging in the park.
This picture helps us counter balance
The days that are too dark
We fly up in the air
Not a care in our souls, hearts or minds.
Dreaming of freedom way up high in the sky
And then we jump into the future and scream.

Jeremiah 29:10-14

For thus says the Lord: Only when Babylon's seventy years are completed will I visit you, and I will fulfill to you my promise and bring you back to this place. For surely I know the plans I have for you, says the Lord, plans for your welfare and not for harm, to give you a future with hope. Then when you call upon me and come and pray to me, I will hear you. When you search for me, you will find me; if you seek me with all your heart, I will let you find me, says the Lord, and I will restore your fortunes and gather you from all the nations and all the places where I have driven you, says the Lord, and I will bring you back to the place from which I sent you into exile.

When in you life did you feel the freedom
and joy of swinging in the park?

What might you do today to bring back that feeling?

DAY TWENTY-THREE

A Poem Called Power

It was a poem called "power." It wasn't even the poem itself. Yet, I was still stopped in my tracks by this one sentence from Cheryl Strayed's book called, ***Wild***.

What is power? Do I have any? Do you?
Power to do what? And why?

Why do we need power?
Why do some people fight and kill for whatever they think power is?

Why do others abhor the word (or what it stands for) and make up new definitions to avoid whatever they believed it had been?

Power? What do I believe lies within that word?

After all it called out to me in a simple sentence. It reached out and grabbed me and caused me to wonder. Five simple letters put together to enthrall, unsettle and perhaps cause me to feel a bit afraid. Afraid of what? I ponder … afraid that I am powerful and powerless all at the same time. I don't have the power to just let this pattern of thought float away.

Perhaps holding on to it is part of the power of this pen I hold and my heart and mind working together.   But then I had to pause because my pen ran out of ink. And in that moment the power shifted or disappeared and my need to write some words became even more powerful. The pull to understand overwhelmed my ability to just let it go. And so I picked up another pen and regained my own special brand of power.   Power that is full of promise and possibility through poetry and prose. I would not be who I am without it. In fact I might all but disappear if I lost the power to ponder over words and wisdom from long ago. I would simply crawl up into a very small ball and never move if the Word was taken from me.

DAY TWENTY-THREE, continued

A Poem Called Power

I don't have the power to just let this pattern of thought float away. Perhaps holding on to it is part of the power of this pen I hold and my heart and mind working together.   But then I had to pause because my pen ran out of ink. In that moment the power shifted or disappeared and my need to write some words became even more powerful. The pull to understand overwhelmed my ability to just let it go. So I picked up a new pen and regained my own special brand of power. Power that is full of promise and possibility through poetry and prose. I would not be who I am without it. In fact, I might all but disappear if I lost the power to ponder over words and wisdom from long ago. I would simply crawl up into a very small ball and never move if the Word was taken from me.

I have come too close to that in my year that was the desert that was San Antonio. In that place and time, I fought for my own sense of power almost without knowing what it was I was fighting for. God offered me power in my weakness through the stories of Jesus. Throughout my life these stories taught me that only through truth can we truly live. Only through forgiveness can we begin to recover, uncover and discover new life again and again. Only in discovering and sharing the gifts we have been given in this life can we become the people we are meant to be.

For me, this world where we struggle around and for and with power is described in *How Great Thou Art*. (Carl Gustav Boberg, 1885) "For Thine is the kingdom and the power and the glory … forever." I am fortunate enough to have this glorious understanding of power fill me up from without and within. And for this I am truly grateful. Amen. Amen. Amen.

How would you answer the questions within this meditation?

DAY TWENTY-FOUR

Mere Majestic Mortals
Yes & No
Both count
Sometimes God says
Never
Not now OR
Wait, just wait
And we don't want to
Wait or not do
So we run in one direction
Or another …
Hither & yon … and we believe
God won't notice that we tried to get away
So God waits because
We can't or
Don't anyway
And then we come to ourselves again
Sometimes we believe
It means that we have found God
But God was never not here
Or there or everywhere
It can't be that we aren't
Part of God
Or even a portion of ourselves
We are always both
Why do we come to think that
A part of us isn't quite true.
That makes no sense –
Not when we stop
And think to understand OR
Be aware of our standing under

DAY TWENTY-FOUR, continued

Mere Majestic Mortals
Standing under and within and
among the angels
or friends who too
are a part of this vast creation
Because all of us partake …
We eat of bread from heaven
Because there is no other type of bread.
All the grain and other ingredients
Come to us from the
Creative force of the universe
Not one can be separate
Even when we set it apart
For our middle supper
We call the last
We all have to eat bread no matter
How it is put together by us
Mere, Majestic Mortals …

Matthew 26:26-28

While they were eating, Jesus took a loaf of bread, and after blessing it he broke it, gave it to the disciples, and said, "Take, eat; this is my body." Then he took a cup, and after giving thanks he gave it to them, saying, "Drink from it, all of you; for this is my blood of the covenant, which is poured out for many for the forgiveness of sins.

Do you believe in the God of all creation?

If not, in what or whom do you put your belief?

DAY TWENTY-FIVE

Life's Paintbrushes

Life's paintbrushes offer us a stroke, a dot or a swirl.
They transform us as we sit and enhance us as we twirl.
So many colors like blue, red or green.
So many shapes still yet to be seen
by me and you and other people too.
The paintbrushes are filled with wishes and sighs.
They cover us up and reveal what's inside.
Paint itself comes in many forms.
It can enhance who we are or discover new norms
To tell us who we are supposed to be.

What colors will you choose
Beyond simple green, red or blue?
Are there purples and pinks or other unexpected hues
Which come forth when we dare
To do more than compare which painting is best
Or too ugly to share?
We all need to see more than what's there
Beyond just one particular scene
Be it filled with yellow, orange or aquamarine.

There's always something waiting to just be revealed.
No one's life is over until our death is sealed.
And even then others add more dabbles on top
So life goes on beating even after a heart has stopped.
Splashes of that and pieces of this
Whirl together to offer us sorrow and bliss.
Each day our picture is surely made new
And a changing frame can offer still a different view
Of who we were when the days hurried past
And our wonderful self is revealed at last.
Not whole, but broken and recreated a bit at a time.
And we pray the whole picture will be more than sublime.

DAY TWENTY-FIVE, continued

Life's Paintbrushes

Proverbs 4:10-27

Hear, my child, and accept my words, that the years of your life may be many. I have taught you the way of wisdom; I have led you in the paths of uprightness. When you walk, your step will not be hampered; and if you run, you will not stumble. Keep hold of instruction; do not let go; guard her, for she is your life.

Do not enter the path of the wicked, and do not walk in the way of evildoers. Avoid it; do not go on it; turn away from it and pass on. For they cannot sleep unless they have done wrong; they are robbed of sleep unless they have made someone stumble. For they eat the bread of wickedness and drink the wine of violence. But the path of the righteous is like the light of dawn, which shines brighter and brighter until full day.

The way of the wicked is like deep darkness; they do not know what they stumble over. My child, be attentive to my words; incline your ear to my sayings. Do not let them escape from your sight; keep them within your heart. For they are life to those who find them, and healing to all their flesh. Keep your heart with all vigilance, for from it flow the springs of life. Put away from you crooked speech, and put devious talk far from you. Let your eyes look directly forward, and your gaze be straight before you. Keep straight the path of your feet, and all your ways will be sure. Do not swerve to the right or to the left; turn your foot away from evil.

What colors describe your life today?

If you could choose new colors, what would they be?

DAY TWENTY-SIX

Ode to the Organ
Circuits & bells
Pedals & swells
What else do you need to make music?
Will it play by itself
Or just sit on a shelf
And never even make a sound?
Stops & Keys
It takes both of these
To create the notes which rise
Out of the pipes of increasing heights
And sometimes offer surprise!
But just sitting alone unlike a phone
The organ won't suddenly start to chime.
No, it takes someone with will
To share knowledge & skill
That makes music others might just call sublime.
We need fingers plus feet
That combine to repeat notes that sit on the page.
So just never let people forget
That a true organ won't play by itself on a stage
Without a mixture of
Circuits & Bells
Pedals & Swells
Along with wisdom, knowhow and courage.

Praise the Lord!

DAY TWENTY-SIX, continued

Ode to the Organ

Psalm 150

Praise God in his sanctuary; praise God in his mighty firmament! Praise God for his mighty deeds; praise God according to his surpassing greatness! Praise God with trumpet sound; praise God with lute and harp! Praise God with tambourine and dance; praise God with strings and pipe! Praise God with clanging cymbals; praise God with loud clashing cymbals! Let everything that breathes praise the Lord!

How do you make music in your life?

What is your favorite type of music?

Do you know why?

DAY TWENTY-SEVEN

Satisfied

What does it mean to be satisfied?
Are we ever full of satisfaction?
Is it OK to just be satisfied
With what we have or who we are?
Seeking to be satisfied with
What I have and who I am.
We are told that God will satisfy us
But then we keep seeking
Instead of just sitting or standing
Or lying down and feeling fully
Satisfied
For who we are
And what we have been given.
So today I will be simply satisfied
And I will savor satisfaction in God.

Psalm 103:1-5

Bless the Lord, O my soul, and all that is within me, bless God's holy name. Bless the Lord, O my soul, and do not forget all God's benefits—who forgives all your iniquity, who heals all your diseases, who redeems your life from the Pit, who crowns you with steadfast love and mercy, who satisfies you with good as long as you live-so that your youth is renewed like the eagle's.

What does it mean to be satisfied?

Are you ever filled with satisfaction?

Is it okay to just be satisfied with what we have or who we are?

DAY TWENTY-EIGHT

Puzzle of Purpose

The Trinity is a puzzle of purpose that's really
beyond our reach.
When the connections are made,
what happens next
is that the Word of God can be preached.
Then the atoms of music and the words of prayer
Point beyond the thresholds of heavenly beams.
So the eyes of the people may be opened
to realize that all persons are connected
through these stories and their dreams.

Matthew 28:16-20

Now the eleven disciples went to Galilee, to the mountain to which Jesus had directed them. When they saw him, they worshipped him; but some doubted. And Jesus came and said to them, 'All authority in heaven and on earth has been given to me. Go therefore and make dis ciples of all nations, baptizing them in the name of the Father and of the Son and of the Holy Spirit, and teaching them to obey everything that I have commanded you. And remember, I am with you always, to the end of the age.'

What is your story for today?

Is there a dream you have not acknowledged?

What would it be?

How might you make your dream come true?

DAY TWENTY-NINE

Pie, Pi

Pie, Pie, we do love pie.
Our love for pie doesn't quite make sense
After all it's made with a few simple ingredients.
Water and flour plus a pinch of salt.
Just pour in a filling to enjoy a delicious result.
Pie is predictable and perfect in real life and dreams
Some favor pie which people call chocolate or coconut crème
There is apple or cherry, pumpkin or berry.
How to decide which is best?
Your decision is never to be taken in jest.
Now there's another pie which describes much of life
Yet it doesn't explain why there's so much strife.
It runs on out in an infinite stream but it's not made of fruit
Or topped with ice cream.
Its ingredients are numbers like three point one four
But as of today there are so many more.
This PI is a number which is said to be real
Yet the things it explains are often surreal
Circles not squares are measured today
By a special ratio or so they say
It's distance around and also across
Any more connections and I'll surely be lost
But to understand PI we have to move beyond logic
Or a rational way.
'Cause its digits don't quite end and never repeat
In any predictable array
This might seem crazy and the terms may be hazy
So if you don't mind I'll stick with my love
For the perfectly rational kind.
Pie, Pie, we do love pie.

DAY TWENTY-NINE, continued

Pie, Pi

Proverbs 1:2-7

For learning about wisdom and instruction, for understanding words of insight, for gaining instruction in wise dealing, righteousness, justice, and equity; to teach shrewdness to the simple, knowledge and prudence to the young—let the wise also hear and gain in learning, and the discerning acquire skill, to understand a proverb and a figure, the words of the wise and their riddles. The fear of the Lord is the beginning of knowledge; fools despise wisdom and instruction.

What is your story for today?

Is there a dream you have not acknowledged?

What would it be?

How might you make your dream come true?

DAY THIRTY

Trinity and Her Ministry
Some of you know this story
For others it's brand new
Perhaps you'll want to listen
as I tell it to you too.

There once was a dog named Trinity
Who went to church each day
She had her own special ministry
Where work was more than play.
She came to live with a preacher lady
Who loves her more than most.
She makes new friends almost every day
But she never likes to boast.
She toddles and smiles around the place
And shares her own special style.
She doesn't bark but likes her treats
And hopes you'll stay awhile.
She plays with the kids, visits the sick
And chases the moonbeams down.
She waits for you whoever you are
To come and see her around.
When you arrive, she'll greet with a nod,
A tail wag and a toy.
The day will seem brighter
As she shares her own special joy.

Dog is God spelled backwards
And God is only love.
So it's not hard to see why Miss Trinity
Has been sent from up above.

DAY THIRTY, continued

Trinity and Her Ministry

1 John 4:7-12

Beloved, let us love one another, because love is from God; everyone who loves is born of God and knows God. Whoever does not love does not know God, for God is love. God's love was revealed among us in this way: God sent his only Son into the world so that we might live through him. In this is love, not that we loved God but that he loved us and sent his Son to be the atoning sacrifice for our sins.

Beloved, since God loved us so much, we also ought to love one another. No one has ever seen God; if we love one another, God lives in us, and his love is perfected in us.

Do you have a pet you love?

Or has your beloved pet gone to heaven'?

Share a story about this pet.

DAY THIRTY-ONE

Musical Ponderings

Music like any other art does not appear out of nothing
It is carried on the wings of a prayer or from the depths of a soul
Notes appear from heartache or wonder
Black and white keys flow together to make magic
Strings or pipes or stops or threads
Vibrate with air to offer beauty
And the silence between the notes gives space
for the ear to hear what years to be said
Where does music begin?
With the angels or the song birds?
Does is arrive with the waves of the oceans
or the crash of an earthquake?
Was music first discovered when a mother
hummed softly to her new born baby?
Or did it appear in an echo across a mountain
Or in the rush of the wind on the plains?
I wasn't there when the first notes
Fluttered from beyond or above.
Perhaps it came from within or through
A moment
So clear that the first note hung in the air
Simply waiting for the next and the next and the next
Until there were chants or hymns or arias
That grew into symphonies and operas
Which filled the earth from top to bottom
and lifted us to the heights of heaven
Or drew us into the horrors of hell
and we listened and heard.
We found
Inspiration and joy.

DAY THIRTY-ONE, continued

Musical Ponderings
We shared tears at the shear magnificence
Of seven notes growing together
Adding sharps or flats and forming
Pictures in our minds and
Movement in our atoms.
Even until our voices joined the chorus of creation
to carry us forward one culture entwining another
So that music passes from generation to generation
And offers a reason to be and believe
Whether music is called sacred or secular
It arises from a place of mystery which compels us
to make even more magical, magnificent,
Miraculous, memorable, mystical music.
For this we say, "Thank you" and even "Amen."

Luke 1:46-50

And Mary said, 'My soul magnifies the Lord, and my spirit rejoices in God my Saviour, for he has looked with favour on the lowliness of his servant. Surely, from now on all generations will call me blessed; for the Mighty One has done great things for me, and holy is his name. His mercy is for those who fear him from generation to generation...'

Where do you hear the angels sing?

What music makes your heart sing?

DAY THIRTY-TWO

Opening the Door

Peace, love & joy once more
As you prepare to open the door
to your life for today.
Will you work or perhaps play on a swing?
Maybe today you will sing
of life and love
while you reach down below
or stretch your arms up above
to discover something forgotten and old.
Or will you hurry forth to live bright and bold?
Is there something you've planned
to encounter, and yet …
you may uncover what you couldn't expect
to find in the middle, beginning or end
of this time in your life.
Perhaps a dream you really won't comprehend
until many moments have passed
the first or the last
thing you remembered to do.
Then meaning will appear
in a memory so clear that you believe
it's what was always intended for you.
Surrounded by peace, joy and love once more
As you prepared to open that beckoning door?

Opening the Door

Revelation 3:8
I know your works. Look, I have set before you an open door, which no one is able to shut. I know that you have but little power, and yet you have kept my word and have not denied my name.

Are you ready for a new door to be opened?

What do you hope to find outside the door?

Who would you invite to come in the door?

Personal Reflections

As you begin a new day, remember to:

Trust God
Do Not Be Afraid
Respect Others Anyway
Give Thanks
Amen

About the Author

Rev. Dr. A. René Whitaker is an ordained Presbyterian minister. She has worked with congregations in transition for 22 years. Rev. Whitaker earned a Master of Divinity at Austin Presbyterian Theological Seminary. In 2014, she completed a Doctor of Ministry in Science and Theology at Pittsburgh Theological Seminary. Her final project is entitled, *Creating Community in a Networked World.*

Rev. Whitaker currently lives in Pennsylvania. She is also available to lead retreats, preach and offer spiritual care. Her first book, *Gravity, Gratitude, Grace: A Journey of Healing & Hope* was published in 2012. Her second book: *Between Time and Meaning* was published in 2016. These were followed by *Enertaining Angels (2017)* along with 88 *Gratitudes: Always Room for More (2018)* which includes reflections on the art of being grateful.